Sonnets of Love and Joy

Poems by

Paul Buchheit

Sonnets of Love and Joy

Poems by

Paul Buchheit

Cover design by Shay Culligan
Cover image *The Love of Paris and Helen*
by Jacques-Louis David (1788)

ISBN: 978-1-63980-363-7

Kelsay Books
502 South 1040 East, A-119
American Fork, Utah 84003
Kelsaybooks.com

EXCERPTED REVIEWS for *Sonnets of Love and Joy:*

Sonnets of Love and Joy by Paul Buchheit shares a collection of poems that reminds us of the beauty of life. The author conjures images that create incredible visuals, whether a storm, sunrise, or other scenes that encourage the imagination.

Sonnets of Love and Joy by Paul Buchheit is a beautiful read that will engage readers with vivid imagery and captivating prose. It's a book of beautiful moments that life gives us.

—Literary Titan

Buchheit combines excellent imagery with graceful structures and original ideas in subjects such as nature, seasons, love, family, friendship, and parenthood. The result is a package of deep, inventive, and dazzling anthologies that offers a luxurious repast for the mind, body, and soul...Buchheit writes with enticing intimacy bringing into his collection the emblem of traditional lyrics that revel in intricacy and formal order.

The poet is such an adroit and keen observer of slight changes in seasons, people, time, and the world in general...mystifying yet elucidating in the manner of a true minstrel...beautiful surreality...[the book] not only desires to be read out loud but also invites reflectivity and heart-searching.

Cruising through this collection is similar to a sumptuous meander through one's favorite gallery linking the distinctive and historical, turning the glass inside and outside, and showcasing Buchheit's masterstroke in his art.

Quill says: Powerful as it is impassioned and forthright, *Sonnets of Love and Joy* by Paul Buchheit flags off the advent of an imperative voice.

—Feathered Quill

This technically polished gathering of sonnets is broad in subject and scope, but consistent in its quality. There is a playful element to the linguistic tangles of this poetic form, and Buchheit leans into that whimsy, particularly in the latter half, with vivid lines and memorable wordplay. This well-curated collection is an emotion-stirring pleasure.

—*Self-Publishing Review*

In this collection, the author will captivate readers with deep and refined sonnets in which vivid images and evocative words abound. There are poets who know how to touch the hearts of their readers with their verses, and this is what happens when one reads *Sonnets of Love and Joy*. Paul Buchheit..masterfully uses words and images to convey emotions a reader rarely feels.

Sonnets of Love and Joy by Paul Buchheit gave me a lot of the joy that is implied in the title. The writing is clean and engaging, with some excellent moments of levity to balance out some of the heavier wording.

Sonnets of Love and Joy..is everything its title suggests and more. The poet has a strong command of the English language and, like Shakespeare, weaves his magic through words, metaphors, and similes. This collection of sonnets is pure joy to read and savor many times over.

—*Readers' Favorite,* 3 reviews

Sonnets of Love and Joy is a collection of sixty sonnets, most of them in Shakespearean form, organized into sections on love, family and friendship, nature, seasons, and the joy of being a child.

The word 'sonnet,' which comes from the Italian word *sonetto* (little song), originated in the 13th century and retained its strict form (14 lines, iambic pentameter, rhyme) through the years of Petrarch and Shakespeare. Modern sonnets, on the other hand, take on diverse forms, with prose, free verse, and even visual poetry. The many variations seem to be an attempt to release the sonnet from a perceived rigidity in form and expression.

But the traditional form need not be restricted in its expressiveness. On the contrary, the meter and rhyme and intelligible language of a carefully crafted "little song" can accentuate the pleasing emotional experience of a poetic reading. It is hoped that *Sonnets of Love and Joy* will provide a few such pleasurable moments.

Contents

Polyhymnia, Charles Meynier (1800)

Love of Another

Two Lovers, Vincent van Gogh (1888)

Loving You

Woman in the Garden Sainte-Adresse, Claude Monet (1867)

A Love Remembered

A melody secreted from the past
is lingering inside me. Neural fires
rekindle, frolic, titillate, and cast
your fleeting image on my eyes. Desires
awaken, musings fill my memory:
your voice and violins, a blossoming
of lovers, lilacs, and the mystery
of woodlands come to life, the early spring
ablush in verdancy, your scented skin
arousing passion in my soul, your smile
an artist's masterpiece as doves begin
to serenade, to flatter and beguile
in waves of soothing choruses, sublime
attendants to my moments back in time.

Native Americans, American Museum Journal (c.1900)

The Mystery That Is You

The gasping hulks of rusted wrecks that share
with eyeless scavengers the mysteries
of Styxlike depths; the lecherous affair
of heaving earth expelling centuries
of fetal carbons from its fiery womb;
grotesque microbic warriors, whose fields
of battle on a wisp of breath consume
great armies, more than all the fallen shields
of kingdoms past; the artisans of stone
and bow, whose boundless hunger would betray
them to a shifting desert bed, where bone
and centuries are ground to chalky gray.
Unseen, like these, the passions that you stirred:
forever in my soul are they interred.

Mountain Bluebird on Seedskadee National Wildlife Refuge

Exquisiteness

The earthen scent of dewy spruce at dawn
unmasks the stormy hours of night. A burst
of tingling misty sun arrives to spawn
the nursling greenery, and soon the first
of purple, pink, and milky spangles blink
beneath the golden haze. A harmony
seduces me: a chippy bobolink
in full command is joined in symphony
by whistle-cheery bluebird rhythms—rise
and fall—and all my senses celebrate
the moment. Then I see your smile, your eyes,
familiar movements that exhilarate
and comfort me, and etch my heart and mind
upon a palette splendidly designed.

Sketch for the painting 'Love,' Jan Ciągliński (1895)

As I See You

Your presence is the sylvan glade aglow
with orchid pinks and marigolds at dawn,
a nightingale as impresario
to orchestras of skittish shadows drawn
to babbling streams, the woodsy sprites
engaged in spurts of chatty merriment.
And like the dawn your vision thrills: it lights
my spirit, sweeps away my discontent.
Your touch entices like the tranquil rains,
your smile invites me to the sultry scent
of willing lips, your voice invokes the strains
of harpists on a sainted instrument.
And if my praises fail, forevermore
will others seek a fitting metaphor.

Julie Le Brun jouant de la guitare, Elisabeth Vigée Le Brun (c.1797)

Succumbing to You

Your playful glance is like a sudden burst
of sun from dreary skies. I'm like a child
enchanted by a rush of colors first
beheld, when some impassioned goddess smiled
at my display of lovestruck innocence.
And now seductive pleasures seem to lift
my spirit to the seraphim, each sense
within me offering a peerless gift.
I taste the airy citrus of the pine
and hear the woodwinds cooing in the stream
and watch the garden's sunlit prisms shine
upon the giddy billows of a dream.
And when you come to me and take my hand,
I'm helpless as a fledgling in the sand.

Cattleya Orchid and Three Hummingbirds, Martin Johnson Heade (1871)

Eternal Search

Upon an autumn stage of fiery gold
arose an orchid, wild and pink, and cream
and puckered, fresh and fair, a blossom bold
as April snow, and stolen from a dream.

But why, thought I, should not such beauty be
embellished in some mystic, distant land
unknown to me? And this I vowed to see,
to feel its blushing presence in my hand.

And so, while fickle moments hurried past,
I conquered every mountain, every shore,
till once around the world I found at last
the precious nectar I was searching for:
abloom and dewy on the woodland floor,
the orchid I beheld so long before.

The Monet Family in Their Garden, Edouard Manet (1874)

Most Beautiful

In praise of *belle arti*: to delight
in *David* and the *Gates of Paradise,*
and *La Giocónda.* Fine pastels ignite
the passions: Fields of lavender entice
the jaded wanderer, *Provénce* astir
amidst the olive greens and burgundies.
Behold the dulcet strains of overture
and aria, from *Carmen,* if it please
the mood, or *La Boheme* or *Figaro.*
For restless vagabond inside of me,
pursuit of beauty conjures such tableau
as these: the artist, vineyard, symphony.
But most sublime, a vision to beguile
my yearning soul, a masterwork, your smile.

Seduction

Love of Another *Seduction*

Susanna and the Elders, Artemisia Gentileschi (c.1630)

Desire

Emerging from the dawn's ambrosial mist
in starry veils from milky galaxies;
seductive as the Satyr in a tryst
with waves voluptuous on surging seas:
her presence coaxes songbirds to rejoice,
her skin is silken, like a cherub's wings,
her lips are passion's reddest fruit, her voice
caressing, comforting, in whisperings
of breezes barely stirring; in her eyes
there burns a black quiescence that defies
surrounding gales, and in her soul the prize
of fires Promethean to tantalize
the courtiers who lust for dawn's reprise
while fevered loins and lyrics agonize.

Lovers, Béla Ványi-Grünwald (1909)

Thirst

Adrift upon the night, a rare perfume
betrays my lover's secrets: she returns
to me in colors bold, an amber bloom
of light upon her skin, as ardor burns
in mine. Partake do I of flavors sweet,
obsessive; unto me her essence pours
seductively, as if she might secrete
her potions as the fitting metaphors
for my imagined feats of derring-do.
Her numbing flows of warmth envelop me
with promise of the rapture to ensue,
with darkness posing as serenity.
In thee, unfailing spirit, I'll confide,
pray not my heated urges should subside!

Madame Gautreau Drinking a Toast, John Singer Sargent (1883)

Intoxicating Lover

A reverie is misted on my mind
like pollen whisked from purple nectaries.
His smile is lustrous, white, as if designed
by deities to cap the churning seas.
The musky bronze perfection of his skin
is closer now, to stir a warlock's brew
of sybaritic turbulence within
me, warming, wooing, lifting me anew
on lips aflame with honeysuckle wine
from Dionysus' vaults. And then I hear
his voice, Satyric strains, and I align
myself with starry musings that appear
upon his presence and enliven me
with blissful visions of our destiny.

The Ironing Maid, Thomas Harrington Wilson (19th Century)

Pubescence

Her blushing scented buxom petals puff
and curtsy through the dusty yellow light,
imposing mischief if I'm bold enough
for scrutiny, and teasing me, contrite
in prurience, succumbing to the brawl
of scrub and suds and flesh and grunt that shocks
pubescent ears and fires a free-for-all
within my Spartan loins, a paradox
of blossomings and battles in my soul
before the domicilic maid-of-war
whose chamber-grooming armaments cajole
me with a hint of matronly decor,
until I'm stirred to taut and tense refrains
to this uplifting keeper of domains.

In the Spirit of Shakespeare

Hope Comforting Love in Bondage, Sidney Harold Meteyard (1901)

When in Disgrace with Fortune

When humbled by disgrace and mocked by fate,
and facing sober destiny alone;
when seraphim no longer celebrate
our union in the rapturous unknown:
begrudged am I of swaggerers' success,
their friends, possessions, wondrous artistry
and boasts of gallantry, while I obsess
on ghosts of vanished skills and certainty.
Yet weighted by the shackles of despair,
my spirit comes alive at thought of you,
when once again the lark is in the air,
my soul and song in welcome rendezvous.
Your presence thrills me like a king's decree
that robes and rubies be our destiny.

Lovers, Auguste Renoir (1875)

Compared to You

How best to celebrate a summer's day?
Comparing it to you, your loveliness,
your warming touch, is like a rose bouquet
that blushes at an intimate caress.
The storms will come, and frigid days await,
as heavenly complexions turn to gray.
When golden hours of summer dissipate
and lure me to the night, I must obey.
But summer shines eternal in your eyes,
your closeness warms my every breath, your smile
compels the smitten gods to agonize
at sight of you, to ravish, to beguile.
In lovely Aphrodite I'll confide:
You've blessed me with Adonis at my side.

Emily's Fairies, E. Gertrude Thomson (1878)

Unspoken Love

Oh love, thou shouldst in jeweled plume exult,
Bedecked blue-green in faerie-winged chiffon,
Or swathed, with pulchritudinous result,
In downy silk and silvers of the swan.
Regardeth thee as blossom of his soul
An epicure of nectar's sweet regale;
Forever doth the desert rose extol
Thy pearls of dawn, to rapturous avail.
So why, to thee, if passion grippeth me
And beggeth praise my spirit to impart,
Doth no avowal bare my fealty,
Or accolade betray my longing heart?
How best to celebrate the morning light?
Above, a feathered hymn in silent flight.

Love and Loss

Rheintöchter, Wilhelm Kray (1828–1889)

Where You Sang to Me

The brooding waves are slapping, lashing, lathering
the oily stubble on the seawall, mossy green
and slick and sinuous, like serpents gathering
from secretive Plutonic depths in some obscene
conspiracy of caterwauling predators
regaling in the devious simplicity
of their disguise. And this is where the troubadours
were lured to you, before a curtain silvery,
a stage of ocean tide. They gazed in ecstasy
upon your face, a white celestial ornament;
their reeds and mandolins were raised in quivery
appeals to steal away your silken instrument.
But now you're gone. And now a brackish probing tongue
consumes the rocky sweetness where your words were sung.

Ariadne Abandoned by Theseus, Angelica Kauffmann (1774)

Love Forsaken

Contentment swathed my soul with silent fires
of rose auroras, till a memory
was harbored deep within. And all desires
of moments yet to come were like a sea
aboil with passion churning, seeking balm
in eyes that held the riddles of the dawn,
their palette rendering my spirit calm
as still-life patterns consummately drawn.

But stir I must as visions fade to gray:
I'm hurled against the frigid, broken shore,
my waves of quietude in disarray.
I'm drowned in oneness, destined to explore
a dimming path of certainties that seem
to teeter on the edges of a dream.

Lost Love, Charles Allston Collins (1828–1873)

Of Love and Loss

The autumn garden gaily beckons me,
with musky earth beneath a fiery show
of scarlet. We're arrayed like royalty
in sunny gold as dawn's fortissimo
of finch and warbler comes to celebrate
our union. Making love with eyes and heart
and reckless passion, longing souls await
completion of a master's work of art.

Now all of life has stilled: I walk alone
amidst the kindred bluebells, lost in swells
of barren musings. Fickle winds intone
uneven harmonies, the crude farewells
of teary deities whose lyrics yearn
for solace when a lover can't return.

Alcibiades on His Knees Before His Mistress,
Louis-Jean-François Lagrenée (1781)

Supplication

I pause amidst a milky galaxy,
a blinding labyrinth in blackened space.
An aching weight, and hint of ecstasy,
conspire to rush me back to your embrace.
How great a fool was I to turn away,
when distances and moments don't exist,
with figments of ethereal display
arranged so blithely for our fevered tryst.
Upon my knees am I, a supplicant
removed of notions brash and starry-eyed.
Assuage my humbled essence with a hint
of moments past—exist they do! . . . my pride
be scorned, berated, banished to this bleak
expanse to shroud a soul so blind, so weak.

Joy of Family and Friends

Doni Tondo, Michelangelo (c.1506)
The Holy Family

Mother and Child, Alice Schille (1916)

My Mother Sang to Me

A minstrel's lyric on a city street
betrays a time long gone, a memory
held captive by a siren's song. Retreat
is my indulgence, to a panoply
of silver maples scattering the sun
upon my eyes like tiny dancing sprites,
the specters of my grizzled beasts undone
by strains from Orpheus and shrill delights
of Pan's seductive reed, the sounds adrift
on fragrant breezes in the melodies
my mother sang to me. And as they lift
me on my wistful passage, and appease
a soul beguiled by scheming Time, I yearn
for blissful days to which I can't return.

Kennedy Long Family, Joshua Johnson (1805)

Siblings

Dear brother, sisters, you're my forest walk
on tranquil pathways, where the scented pine
has stirred my senses, where the breezes talk
in whispers and the songbirds build a shrine
to winged ensembles in the greenery.

I begged of Flora on my woodland trail:
Oh guardian of orchids, deign to free
your dainty handmaids for a fairy tale
of pink perfection on our journeyway.

She heard, and now, dear siblings, I can feel
our kinship. Let your sympathies allay
my fears, your gentle humor still appeal
to me as years depart, your caringness
remind me of the fortunes I possess.

Photograph, Allen Ayrault Green (1880–1963)

Oldest Friend

I breathe the aging pine and crumbling walls,
where gramps and I would while away the dusk,
regaled by peeper frogs and peppy calls
of whip-poor-wills beneath the woodsy musk
that hovered in the gloom. I see his face,
like drought on furrowed earth, tobacco stains
on checkered shirt, a coarse guffaw, a trace
of mischief in his manner as he feigns
amusement at some nonsense from a child.
A gruff and grizzled man, but dignified,
a patriarch, a kin to forest wild,
betrothed to home and memories. Beside
his empty rocking chair, I sit and stare
at fading skies, at nights we used to share.

Two People on the Way to the Forest, Edvard Munch (1884)

To an Old Friend

Along the restless journeyway I chance
upon a long-abandoned memory:
deserted now, a beggarly expanse
of timeworn brush and bramble. Hurriedly
I pass it by. But just ahead a road
once shared with you, still flush with pinkish light
and moist with swelling soils, where boughs explode
with blossoms, *Rose of Sharon,* to invite
my fancy. Old and new, our paths converge
in winding escalade above a haze
of *Fauna's* silken breath, and they emerge
beneath the grandest summit's snowy blaze.
Sensations pleasant, proud, return to me:
again I share the finest company.

Two Men Contemplating the Moon, Caspar David Friedrich (c.1825)

To a Friend Most Dear

Abandoned not am I in bully winds
that slap in broken rhythms at my face;
nor cast to sea, where sulking origins
of primal darkness gather to embrace
departing souls; nor muted and forlorn
upon the spinning bluish desert heat.
Instead a lyricist's refrains adorn
the calm repentant air; in swift retreat
are masters of the sea, their tridents shorn
and spirited away; and from the sands
afire with dirges is a Phoenix born
and lifted skyward in protective hands:
all flourish in the boundlessness and bliss
of friendship rare, and ours is such as this.

Merry Trio, Judith Leyster (c.1630)

Remembering an Unconventional Friend

These trodden paths are pleasant, so we pass, again, again.
Familiarity emboldens us, we spurn the roads
for now and start upon the byways, black and silent; then
we scurry back in laughter's keep to cling to sweet abodes.

A shad'wy figure passes by, adventurer or fool?
For of a ghostly still, a dusky gray, a numbing chill,
an untried way, he is a part; not fear or ridicule
deter him from his whims and roves, from doing what he will.

And then he's gone. A taunting autumn bluster slaps at me,
evoking shivers as I stand before the path he took.
To shelter, wisely, I withdraw, relieved I'm not to see
the ill beyond, but wishing for the recklessness to look.

When smoky dawn obscures the path I traveled yesterday,
I contemplate how hurriedly the time has passed away.

The Thankful Poor, Henry Ossawa Tanner (1894)

A Shared Path

A quest elusive as the mythical
Olympus, Sisyphean is my path,
like crumbling parchment, brooding obstacle
of blackness in a bestial grip, the wrath
of stone behemoths shedding sun-dried skin,
and ponderous the solitude that looms
ahead. But then a voice! Like violin,
such soothing strains; like mist of rare perfumes
that quench the fiery air; like veils of dust
that fashion spangled stairway panoplies,
until from Àeolus a rhythmic gust
elicits welcome from the deities,
and secrets of my fortune they intone:
be firm your path, but venture ne'er alone.

Les Alyscamps, Avenue in Arles, Vincent van Gogh (1888)

To Live Not Alone

From dusty lifeless earthen crusts emerge
entangled webs of supple limbs, ahush
with secrets in their lifeblood, on the verge
of dawning, ravenously poised to gush
with glossy jades of haughty innocence
in countless sprouted testaments, embraced
and blazoned by the rays of Providence,
celestial strings and satins interlaced.

But like the leafy spirits, left alone
we wither, flutter, crumble, and exist
no more, returning to the soil, our throne
the lap of phantoms in a faceless mist.

Unfettered by the starry-white facade,
we tumble from the palette of a god.

Best Friends, Romualdo Locatelli (1934)

Finest Part of Life

A fleeting rush of wonder, like the scent
of April hyacinth, beguiles my mind
with sweet cajolery for sentiment
about the greater good of humankind.

Are riches key? A king's bijouterie?
The splendid pleasure domes of Xanadu?
The blissful flush of notoriety,
the gushing tribute of a retinue?
A peacock flaunting feathery to weave
a tapestry of courtship? Or the prize
of life hereafter, yearning to achieve
the spirit world? 'Tis best to recognize
the noblest attribute of humankind
as valued friendship never left behind.

Joy of Nature

Meeting by the River, Robert Seldon Duncanson (1864)

Sky Study with Birds, Jean-Michel Cels (1842)

On Becoming One

In whispers comes a fluttering of wings,
a pair of snowy specks on azure skies.
Rebelliously a trembly aspen clings
to mirthful breezes with a faint reprise,
and breathes the flutist's airy heralding
of reckless synchrony. The wings of snow
are teasing now: their soundless sweepings bring
a spiraling of white, a flirting glow
against the woodland in a single wave
of plummeting and pause, a harmony
of elegance as artisans engrave
an etching on the blue, a symphony
of silence in the bounty of the sun
as kindred lives exult, becoming one.

Waterfall with Birches, unknown author (19th century)

Pleasantries at Dusk

A wispy ticklish dewy flow of mist
arises from the churning waterfall,
as goldenrod assemble in a tryst
with bluebells, and the chickadees enthrall
their audience with cheery melodies.
Along the bubbly stream staccato flows
of glitter gurgle through the fallen trees,
and cattails mobilize in stoic rows
like darkened fingers of a phantom-like
creation first ascending from the womb.
At touch of dusk these puckish wonders strike
a chord of passion in the black perfume
of dampened earth, a sensual delight
that lingers far beyond approaching night.

Coucher de soleil, ciel orange, Félix Vallotton (1910)

Homage to Orange

Behold the brilliant bird of paradise,
aglow at sunset with chrysanthemums
and marigolds competing to entice
the wanderer who helplessly succumbs
to ginger-tinged seductions. Come the night
a pageantry of flame illuminates
the canopy of maples, which delight
again when blush of daybreak penetrates
the arborland. When worlds were formed the Muse
and rainbow goddess Iris was implored:
Emblazon us with iridescence, choose
your most revered and vibrant hue! She poured
an orangish nectar from a jug, then rose
to flaunt herself in versicolored pose.

Palo Duro Canyon, Georgia O'Keeffe (1917)

Horizons, Dusk to Dawn

Seductive grassy waves, the *dance of veils,*
arouse my languid spirit. Stolen fires
ignite the dusk, Prometheus regales
the earth as chaff is cast upon the pyres,
the lustrous ambers on a scimitar
of scarlet, slicing patterns in my mind,
till blackness seethes from sulking depths to blur
the handiwork of gods. And in the blind
hurrahs of dawn, with breezes slapping dry
and chilling harbingers of savagery
to come, my musings coax an alibi
of pinkish blush amidst a stagnant sea
of mountain peaks that muscle from the gloom,
deferring storms in airs of rose abloom.

Landscape with the Fall of Icarus, Joos de Momper the Younger (1564–1635)

Celestial Dream

The faintest drumbeat, then a moment's pause,
a murmuring of Siren voices, strains
of cherubs cooing with polite applause
as Icarus, of crippled wing, abstains
from fiery fantasies. But swept away
am I by flights of fancy to the womb
that raised me to the sun, a passageway
to barely opened eyes, the air abloom
in musky sweetness, languid dust afloat
like tiny buoys on the warming waves
from yellowed windows. And the skies emote
with longing as a soulful hum engraves
its cadence on my mind, embracing whims
that lure me back to childhood seraphims.

Impression: Sunrise, Claude Monet (1872)

Dawnlight

The sunlight on the icy riverbed
reflects like phantoms flitting from a trail
of jewels, satinlike, a silver thread
of timid dawn embossing milky-pale
and heaving floes. I turn to savor streams
of bluish apparitions, blackened spruce
surrendering to daylight, dogged beams
of light encroaching, hoping to seduce
a softening to woodsy scents. And flushed
with vigor, gangs of glitter skirt away
with buntings on the frost, and in their rushed
ascent to solitude a lush bouquet
of whitish puffings flutter from the pine,
in grand arrays of Helios' design.

Wheat Field in Rain, Vincent van Gogh (1889)

Evening Rain

With skips and stops a droplet trickles down
my dusty window in the grudging light
of purple dusk. Of dubious renown,
I ponder, came to be this teary sprite:
once beaded on the gritty, steaming flesh
of men constructing temples at the whim
of emperors; once pinkish spray as fresh
incisions from a lash enacted grim
formalities; once moistening the eyes
and trembling fingers of a wizened squaw
whose sacred lands and people faced demise
amidst the tumult of a scornful law.
And now returns this relic to restore
its long-forgotten past, to live once more.

Songbirds in a Woodland Marsh, Fidelia Bridges (1879)

Harmonies

The chirpy wheedling of a thrush invites
me to the dewy gardenscape at dawn.
I savor hints of pine: a finch alights,
all fidgety and flirty, but he's gone
in practiced whispers. Then a raucous call,
a jealous jay announcing that the space
belongs to him. The morning protocol
resumes, as callers tunefully embrace
my quiet presence. Now a yellow flash,
the whistly greeting of a warbler, shrill,
falsetto. I reflect upon my brash
companions of the homestead, how they thrill,
as I, at tickling mist and pinkish skies,
a time for each of us to fantasize.

Monet Painting in His Garden, Pierre-Auguste Renoir (1873)

To See the Splendor

I breathed the dewy earth a thousand dawns,
beside the courtly trellises adorned
with yellow roses, freshly scented lawns,
the choruses of doves that cooed and mourned
to spell the songbirds, and the fledgling plum,
in burgundy or brown or fiery red,
bequeathed by season's hymn. And I succumb
again to battlefields of sparrows spread
among the glitter-dizzied leafy shields
of poplar. Pixie pin-prick kisses spray
my cheeks, an airy breath of balsam yields
a teasing hint of citrus. Every day
I hurry past to matters critical,
though none upon this dawn seem meaningful.

A Boy Walking through a Danish Wood, Hans Agersnap(1857–1925)

On Passing Through the Morning Woods

On spirits skittish as a trail of smoke
upon the breeze, I summon up the dawn
in orangish bites of juniper and oak
and chilly tinglings on my skin. I'm drawn
to sunny scatterings that stutter through
the whisp'ry thicket, where familiar rhymes
untangle glassy-mottled residue
of waking mind with quirky pantomimes
of woodland sprites, and in the forestscape
I'm but a will-o'-wisp, a leaf let free
in reveries of silence, spectral shape
against the swarthy spruce, my destiny
on spinning skies, the harmony begun,
and all the earth a mother to her son.

Stormy Landscape, Rembrandt (1638)

Storm

A stirring in the oak, a tomblike pause,
and then a rhythmic misty harmony
is tapping on the leaves, as if applause
were heralding some heavenly esprit
for boughs awakened by the winds. A veil
of steamy gloom obscures the arborland,
and droplets in neurotic fits impale
me to the pathway seeking reprimand,
and from the heavens plummet raucous sheets
of rushing tumult in a foamy swell
of whiteness as a vengeful god excretes
a burst of venom to the depths of hell.
In awe I watch this act of Providence:
it renders impotent my every sense.

Storm in the Mountains, Albert Bierstadt (1870)

After the Storm: A Moment of Peace

I'm swathed in velvet silence, silken, smooth,
with silver rippled monograms of dawn
between the peaks, where breezes poised to soothe
me with a lover's touches are withdrawn
by jealous deities who choose to press
against my ears the hum of centuries
of woodland meditations. But they bless
me with this stillness, with the panoplies
of spellbound apparitions in the leaves,
and colors rendered by an artist's brush,
and feathered coteries that one perceives
as whimsy till a strident cry and rush
of wings reveals their moment of caprice
to be the shattered fragments of my peace.

Rembrandt Laughing, Rembrandt (c.1628)

Joy of Life

How serendipitous to be alive!
A bauble on a mountain can be found
before the boundless seeds of life connive
to raise a single palette to the ground
to paint your portrait. And a drop of rain
will overflow the seas before a bed
of ancient lovers dares to preordain
your claim to life a million years ahead.

So gather rose and honey, taste the scent
of pine in daybreak's satin hues, delight
in murmurings of starlings' swift ascent,
and bathe in milky riddles of the night.

And welcome every touch and fond embrace,
the living gestures of your earthly space.

Joy of the Seasons

Paysage, Berthe Morisot (1867)

Winter Moment

The silent flakes of snow, like dainty white
and flitting whimsies in a frenzied quest
to join as one, unerringly alight
upon my path, as if at my behest.

The odor, sweet, of burning maple curls
through thickened flurry walls; a wolflike whine
betrays the gale arising as it swirls
and bullies through the tips of stubborn pine.

The cabin beckons me; a dullish light
prepares me for a welcome interlude
of warmth and sustenance, an age-old rite,
an intercourse of fire and solitude.

The wintry pomp and bluster need not cease,
for in my womblike refuge I'm at peace.

Indian Woman Moccasin Seller, Cornelius Krieghoff (1815–1872)

Together on a Snowy Path

A silv'ry flicker through the silent pine
has stirred us: she, engulfed in puffery
of snowball white, convinced the nightlong whine
of wolfish winds has carved a pageantry
of stony icescapes just beyond our womb
of crackling hearth. Outside, the blush of dawn
is on her skin; the smoky sweet perfume
of maple wafts and withers, here and gone.
She shoes ahead through rows of slumping pine,
their cotton boughs against the blue, like stairs
erected by a heavenly design.
She turns and smiles, and all the world declares
an instant of perfection in her eyes,
as pearly snowbanks sparkle in reprise.

The Christmas Tree, Albert Chevallier Tayler (1911)

Winter Celebration

The regal bearing of a Norway pine,
in bluish green attire, a scent of mint,
and sculptured by a scriptural design,
adorns the Christmas parlor with a hint
of arrogance. And when the revelry
begins, the icon beckons, standing tall
and teasingly aglow, its mystery
like that of kings, its bearing to recall
the promises of harmony among
its fairy-eyed idolaters. I turn
to step outside, to feel the breath of young
and fragrant conifers that seem to yearn
for balm and shelter with a burning sense
of right, like children bathed in innocence.

Sous-bois, Paul Cézanne (c.1890)

Spring Awakening

The sulking landscape, brittle, dreary, stained
with clutter like an airless alleyway,
ignites in fleeting brilliance, as if deigned
by Ceres that the heavens might display
a brushstroke's dabbled hint of virgin green
as prelude to a symphony of change.
In sudden rustlings playful sprites convene
in chatty complement to rearrange
their homestead; and a prankish sparrow swoons
and darts and teases; and a scheming squall,
whose grudging bitter grip, in rasping tunes
through weary pine, once dared to taunt and brawl,
acknowledges its weakening affair
by lifting faint hosannas to the air.

Spring Spreads One Green Lap of Flowers, John William Waterhouse (1910)

A Stirring in the Soil

On scented earth, a reawakening
occurs beneath the haunts of winter snow,
in musty waves, as if a blossoming
of crocuses might suddenly bestow
their purplish charms on long-suspended dreams.
The sunlight scatters shadows on my skin:
a ghostly palette with a thousand themes
to paint upon my mind. From deep within
my soul I revel in a murmuring
of starlings on the glassy monolith
of livened skies. And now the flittering
response of skittish air fulfills the myth
of Zephyrus, who offers up the prize
of newborn greenery before my eyes.

Cherry Tree in Blossom, Edvard Munch (1905)

Lovely as a Tree in Spring

I feel the wintry fingers ease their grip.
Think spring! . . . an urging from the chickadees
that peppy mates should join in fellowship.
I greet the wood: impatient redbud trees
shall soon be christened with the sweetened scents
ne'er known to tethered souls. So walk with me,
see beauty in these godly testaments,
a blessing from the lord of fantasy,
poem-maker, proud *Silvanus* flaunting spring
as cloak of gentle green, and counseling:
Love lea or heath, but pleasures none can bring
as does the woodland! Hear the Muses sing
a tribute borne of wing and Providence:
Tree, praise to thee! We bow, with reverence.

Summer Sunshine, Numa François Gillet (1868–1940)

Share with Me the Start of Summer

A leafy rustling, cooling piny breeze,
a misting breath and reassuring voice,
earth's keeper with her child. I feel at ease
beneath a speckled canopy, my choice
for shelter from the searing brilliant white
expanse, while woodsy glimmer flickers through
the clotted overgrowth in hurried flight,
avoiding timbered hands to rendezvous
on mossy paths. I hear a whispering
of sorts: a sleepy humming monotone
regales me with a warmish glowering
that gathers on the earth like heavy stone.
And on and on such hymns and litanies,
till weary witness nightfall might appease.

A wooded path in autumn, H. A. Brendekilde (1902)

On Greeting the Splendors of Autumn

The flirting winds are slapping at my face,
while silver scatterings of daylight slip
and stutter through the arbor to embrace
my silent praise. I find companionship
with crimson leaflets flashing impish bits
of flighty motion. Gentle rustlings stir
the forest floor - a forager emits
directives in a fuss of chirp and fur.

The musky pathway seeks communion with
the bluebells and the roaming rods of gold,
all spilled in starry tales of ancient myth
when Flora, bearing gifts, was first cajoled.

And I'm a shadow on a charmed abode,
a will-o'-wisp upon a wishing road.

From the U.S. Fish and Wildlife Service

As Seasons Pass: Brief Is Life

With secrets rustling through the winter oak
and echoes on primeval forest floor
come palpitating rains. A thunderstroke
foretells the whitish glowing metaphor
of dastardly Promethean bequest:
the earth convulsing in a flaming gasp,
then crumbling dry, like mysteries suppressed
in ancient tombs. But chilling breezes grasp
the aftermath with glowering lament,
the sleet lays willow switches on my face,
and scowling swirls of white in swift descent
defy the weary huntress to embrace
her tumbling cubs before the bitter cold
intensifies the dark a thousandfold.

Joy of Children

One Hundred Children in the Long Spring, Su Hanchen (c.1130–1160)

Birth, Hannah Hoch (1924)

First Moments

Afloat on billowings of spectral seas
and oozing blackish matter, pirouettes
of vapor dizzy me as spirits squeeze
me through the smooth facade; and brawling jets
of steam are heaving, thrusting, bellowing
grotesquely grunted gurglings . . . now a blue
and silv'ry icy blast is buffeting
my dripping skin . . . and now a great to-do:
a gaudy spectacle of pink and green
emits a warmish shrill cacophony
of voices cradling me with velveteen
and woolly coverings. Serenity
embraces me, at last, with comely charms,
with breath and essence in my mother's arms.

Child with a Dog, Francis Wheatley (1747–1801)

Moments with My Grandchild

A giggling princess, ticklish puppy licks,
and playful glints of sunrise fill the air
to rouse my idle mind, to nimbly fix
the fleeting moment in the watchful stare
of forest goddesses who ride a wave
of rosy scents enhanced by evergreen,
while urging jaunty thrushes to engrave
their cheery message on a woods pristine.

Upon this balmy haze of innocence,
in kinship with a rapturous parade
of pearly ripples on the stream, intense
emotions flood my mind and serenade
my child and me with gentle rhapsodies
of joy that seem to linger on the breeze.

The Artist's Garden at Vétheuil, Claude Monet (1881)

Child's Garden

To never end, we thought, the morning light
that kissed our eyes, and breezes whispering
with cherub voices, pausing to invite
us to a secret world, and conjuring
the whims of pussy willow magic wands
and piney beds for tiny acrobats
and games of hide and seek in grassy fronds
above our heads, where growls of jungle cats
are tamed to laughter by a kindly oak
who lowers crooked fingers in support,
as dandelion parachutes evoke
a frantic chase, and milky clouds exhort
celestial palettes to intensify
the carnival of shapes upon the sky.

Picking Flowers in a Field, Mary Cassatt (1875)

Remembering Father's Garden

The garden girds for spring with purples, pinks,
and lacy bluebells. Daddy always near,
with teasing words and reassuring winks
as fingers black and fussing disappear
beneath a nursery of soil to coax
the precious start of life from needy sprites
of marigolds. The earthy stir evokes
a host of warnings from disrupted flights
of nervous crows; and daddy turns to tend
his brood. But mine's a world of pixie dust
that slowly casts a spell: while I pretend
the day is young, the man to whom I trust
my dreams becomes my shepherd and my squire
amidst a fading night's cicada choir.

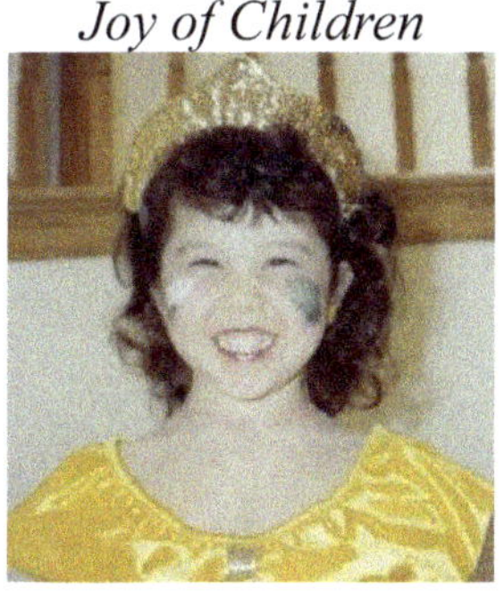

Daughter

My pixie snowgirl, pink and cheeky pout
and bubbly giggles lifting her above
the clouds, where cherubs fill the roundabout
with candle-flicker eyes and turtle dove
caressings, sparking neural tickling fires
inside me. On my lap a dawning mind,
a word and letter toolbox that aspires
to build foundations for her castles lined
with knights and damsels. From another room
I hear her rhymes ascend to mythical
companions in her storybooks, on plume
of sweetest songbird, as a gardenful
of gentle fauna seek to understand
this dainty daughter of a fairyland.

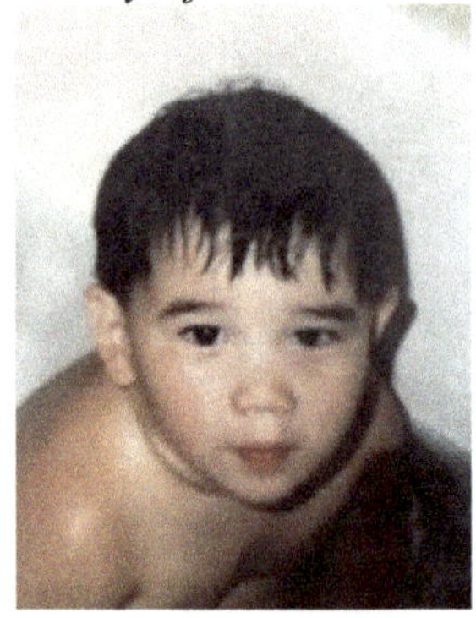

Son

All bouncy, waggy, and inquisitive,
the little boy behind the puckish grin;
and puppy prankish, always positive
in spirit, cubby huggable, and kin
to sprites and soulmates in his restless mind.
He travels on the breezes to a land
of kings and noblemen secured behind
their swordsmen, where his boyish contraband
abounds with games and mischief and refrains
of knightly skirmishes on carousels,
and jesters, magic acts, and circus trains,
and heroes, scalawags, and ne'er-do-wells.
And all the triumphs on his well-worn trail
will be another schoolboy's fairy tale.

Children's Games, Pieter Brueghel the Elder (c.1560)

Before School

The schoolyard comes alive with gleeful shrieks,
a rainbow splash of candy-coated blurs,
like pinwheels, twirling, echoing with squeaks
and screeches as a purple creature stirs,
with tangled tubes and platforms that expel
the tots in reckless waves, electron-like,
in blinks and twinkles. Then a warning bell
impertinently sounds: a startled tyke
obeys the call to calm and halts before
tin soldier figures of authority,
and silence ripples, like the forest floor
in waning winds. A jaunty memory
remains: the tiny voices, fancy-free,
in whirling wheels of frenzied harmony.

Dancing Children, Helen Sophia O'Hara (1900)

Recess

The schoolhouse door is opened, children burst
outside, as if a dreary brick machine
had come to life and suddenly disbursed
the pieces of a puzzle, to careen
and bounce in random spasms of delight,
to pop and puff like puppets come alive,
like colored corn and little trinkets bright
as stars, while cream and sugar clouds arrive
to shade the bubble blue of oxygen
that fuels the wildfire. Fairy stories turn
from page to page as shadows skip and spin,
celestial flames continuing to burn
until they settle, cradled and content
inside, like angel faces, heaven-sent.

Carousel, Vilmos Aba-Novák (1931)

Merry-Go-Round

The mirth and titter from the carousel;
the barker's calls, the clangs and spinning wheels;
the tots, like pinballs, to and fro; the smell
of popcorn, donuts, beer; the sassy squeals
of bottle-toppling winners; and the swirls
of fluffy pink and gooey gossamer,
the little sticky-fingered boys and girls,
each one a ne'er-do-well adventurer.

The day retreats to hints of Wonderland,
like Alice in the grass, the cumulus
adrift against the azure blue in grand
displays of cotton candy shapes, the fuss
and bother of the world a thousand miles
away, beyond the children's sleepy smiles.

The Swimming Hole, Charles Courtney Curran (c.1894)

Summer Dream

The pier awakens with a cheery squeal,
a rowdy waterspray of whirlwind blurs,
chaotic blinks of sun above a peal
of laughter as a wooden creature stirs,
its stumpy fingers ready to expel
the children one by one in popcorn pops,
an endless spinning splashing carousel
of tag and tussle, flips and belly flops.

As downy feather clouds caress the sky,
obliging hands of time are standing still,
and chatty breezes seem to testify
to certainties of childhood dreams, the thrill
of sun-borne flights to worlds of fancy-free
in bursts of blue and bubbly harmony.

A Young Girl and Her Dog, Joshua Reynolds (c. 1780)

Pup in Heaven

A maiden stands beside her friend, as evening mist
begins to slip and spirit through the cheery lights
of days that seemed forever. Sleepy eyes resist
the pixie dust and kisses of celestial sprites.
The maiden calls—a moment's fuss, her little friend
is in her arms; they gather for a rendezvous
with playmates in a castle garden. They ascend
beyond the realms of valiant knights and derring-do
to cotton billows frolicking upon the sky
in images of lambs at pasture lulled to sleep.
And gentle laughter, softer than a lullaby,
is carried to the winds below, as if to keep
a vision in the air: a little girl, a pup,
a starry romp, and angels barely keeping up.

Image Credits

COVER
The Love of Paris and Helen by Jacques-Louis David (1788)
https://commons.wikimedia.org/wiki/File:Les_Amours_de_P%C3%A2ris_et_d%27H%C3%A9l%C3%A8ne,_David,_1788.jpg
COVER (Inside)
Polyhymnia, Charles Meynier (1800)
https://commons.wikimedia.org/wiki/File:Polyhymnia,_Muse_of_Eloquence_-_Charles_Meynier.jpg

I. LOVE OF ANOTHER
Two Lovers, Vincent van Gogh (1888)
https://commons.wikimedia.org/wiki/File:Van_Gogh_-_Liebespaar_in_Arles_(Ausschnitt).jpeg
A Love Remembered
Woman in the Garden Sainte-Adresse, Claude Monet (1867)
https://commons.wikimedia.org/wiki/File:Monet,_Claude_-_Woman_in_the_Garden._Sainte-Adresse.jpg
The Mystery That Is You
Native Americans, American Museum Journal (c.1900)
https://commons.wikimedia.org/wiki/File:The_American_Museum_journal_(c1900-(1918))_(18133607766).jpg
Exquisiteness
Mountain Bluebird on Seedskadee National Wildlife Refuge
https://commons.wikimedia.org/wiki/File:Mountain_Bluebird_on_Seedskadee_National_Wildlife_Refuge_(25610552823).jpg
As I See You
Sketch for the painting 'Love,' Jan Ciągliński (1895)
https://commons.wikimedia.org/wiki/File:Jan_Ci%C4%85gli%C5%84ski_-_Sketch_for_the_painting_%E2%80%9CLove%E2%80%9D_-_MP_1759_MNW_-_National_Museum_in_Warsaw.jpg
Succumbing to You
Julie Le Brun jouant de la guitare, Elisabeth Vigée Le Brun (c.1797)
https://commons.wikimedia.org/wiki/File:Elisabeth_Vig%C3%A9e_Le_Brun_-_Julie_Le_Brun_jouant_de_la_guitare.jpg
Eternal Search
Cattleya Orchid and Three Hummingbirds, Martin Johnson Heade (1871)
https://commons.wikimedia.org/wiki/File:Martin_Johnson_Heade-Cattleya_Orchid_and_Three_Brazilian_Hummingbirds.jpg

Most Beautiful
The Monet Family in Their Garden, Edouard Manet (1874)
https://www.metmuseum.org/art/collection/search/436965
Desire
Susanna and the Elders, Artemisia Gentileschi (c.1630)
https://commons.wikimedia.org/wiki/File:Artemisia_Gentileschi_-_Susanna_and_the_Elders_NOT_NCMG_1964_77.jpg
Thirst
Lovers, Béla Iványi-Grünwald (1909)
https://commons.wikimedia.org/wiki/File:Iv%C3%A1nyi_Lovers_1909.jpg
Intoxicating Lover
Madame Gautreau Drinking a Toast, John Singer Sargent (1883)
https://commons.wikimedia.org/wiki/File:Madame_Gautreau_Drinking_a_Toast.jpg
Pubescence
The Ironing Maid, Thomas Harrington Wilson (19th Century)
https://commons.wikimedia.org/wiki/File:Thomas_Harrington_Wilson_The_ironing_maid.jpg
When in Disgrace with Fortune
Hope Comforting Love in Bondage, Sidney Harold Meteyard (1901)
https://commons.wikimedia.org/wiki/File:Sidney_Harold_Meteyard_-_Hope_Comforting_Love_in_Bondage_-_1948P5_-_Birmingham_Museums_Trust.jpg
Compared to You
Lovers, Auguste Renoir (1875)
https://commons.wikimedia.org/wiki/File:Pierre-Auguste_Renoir_068_(Les_amoureux).jpg
Unspoken Love
Emily's Fairies, E. Gertrude Thomson (1878)
https://commons.wikimedia.org/wiki/File:Emily%27s_Fairies_WA_MVAS.jpeg
Where You Sang to Me
Rheintöchter, Wilhelm Kray (1828–1889)
https://commons.wikimedia.org/wiki/File:Wilhelm_Kray_-_Rheint%C3%B6chter_-_9198_-_Bavarian_State_Painting_Collections.jpg
Love Forsaken
Ariadne Abandoned by Theseus, Angelica Kauffmann (1774)
https://commons.wikimedia.org/wiki/File:Angelica_Kauffmann,_Ariadne_Abandoned_by_Theseus,_1774.jpg

Of Love and Loss
Lost Love, Charles Allston Collins (1828–1873)
https://commons.wikimedia.org/wiki/File:Charles_Allston_Collins_-_Lost_Love.jpg
Supplication
Alcibiades on his Knees Before his Mistress, Louis-Jean-François Lagrenée (1781)
https://commons.m.wikimedia.org/wiki/File:Lagrenee_-_Alcibiades_on_his_Knees_Before_his_Mistress_-_c.1781.jpg

II. JOY OF FAMILY AND FRIENDS
Doni Tondo, Michelangelo (c.1506)
The Holy Family
https://commons.wikimedia.org/wiki/File:Michelangelo,_tondo_doni_02.jpg
My Mother Sang to Me
Mother and Child, Alice Schille (1916)
https://commons.wikimedia.org/wiki/File:Alice_Schille_128_Porto_Rican_Mother_and_Child.jpg
Siblings
Kennedy Long Family, Joshua Johnson (1805)
https://commons.wikimedia.org/wiki/File:Kennedy_Long_Family_by_Joshua_Johnson.jpg
Oldest Friend
Photograph by Allen Ayrault Green (1880–1963)
https://commons.wikimedia.org/wiki/File:Old_man_with_boy_(NBY_23).jpg
To an Old Friend
Two People on the Way to the Forest, Edvard Munch (1884)
https://commons.wikimedia.org/wiki/File:Munch_-_To_p%C3%A5_vei_mot_skogen_(Couple_on_the_Path_to_the_Forest),_lot.213_(cropped).jpg
To a Friend Most Dear
Two Men Contemplating the Moon, Caspar David Friedrich (c.1825)
https://commons.wikimedia.org/wiki/File:Caspar_David_Friedrich_045_light.jpg
Remembering an Unconventional Friend
Merry Trio, Judith Leyster (c.1630)
https://commons.wikimedia.org/wiki/File:Judith_Leyster_Merry_Trio.jpg

A Shared Path
The Thankful Poor, Henry Ossawa Tanner (1894)
https://commons.wikimedia.org/wiki/File:The_Thankful_Poor,_1894._Henry_Ossawa_Tanner.jpg
To Live Not Alone
Les Alyscamps, Avenue in Arles, Vincent van Gogh (1888)
https://commons.wikimedia.org/wiki/File:Vincent_van_Gogh_-_Les_Alyscamps_(Goulandris_Foundation).jpg
Finest Part of Life
Best Friends, Romualdo Locatelli (1934)
https://commons.wikimedia.org/wiki/File:Best_Friends_-_Romualdo_Locatelli.jpg

III. JOY OF NATURE
Meeting by the River, Robert Seldon Duncanson (1864)
https://commons.wikimedia.org/wiki/File:Meeting_by_the_River_by_Robert_Seldon_Duncanson,_1864.jpg
On Becoming One
Sky Study with Birds, Jean-Michel Cels (1842)
https://commons.wikimedia.org/wiki/File:Jean-Michel_Cels_-_Sky_study_with_birds.jpg
Pleasantries at Dusk
Waterfall with Birches, unknown author (19th century)
https://commons.wikimedia.org/wiki/File:Waterfall_with_Birches.jpg
Homage to Orange
Coucher de soleil, ciel orange, Félix Vallotton (1910)
https://commons.wikimedia.org/wiki/File:F%C3%A9lix_Vallotton_-_Sonnenuntergang,_orangefarbener_Himmel.jpeg
Horizons, Dusk to Dawn
Palo Duro Canyon, Georgia O'Keeffe (1917)
https://commons.wikimedia.org/wiki/File:Georgia_O%27Keeffe,_Palo_Duro_Canyon,_1916-1917.tif
Celestial Dream
Landscape with the Fall of Icarus, Joos de Momper the Younger (1564–1635)
https://commons.wikimedia.org/wiki/File:Landscape_with_the_Fall_of_Icarus_(Joos_de_Momper_d.y.)_-_Nationalmuseum_-_17734.tif

Dawnlight
Impression: Sunrise, Claude Monet (1872)
https://commons.wikimedia.org/wiki/File:Claude_Monet,_Impression,_soleil_levant,_1872.jpg
Evening Rain
Wheat Field in Rain, Vincent van Gogh (1889)
https://commons.wikimedia.org/wiki/File:Wheat_Field_in_Rain_-_My_Dream.jpg
Harmonies
Songbirds in a Woodland Marsh, Fidelia Bridges (1879)
https://commons.wikimedia.org/wiki/File:Songbirds_in_a_Woodland_Marsh,_Fidelia_Bridges.jpg
To See the Splendor
Monet Painting in His Garden, Pierre-Auguste Renoir (1873)
https://commons.wikimedia.org/wiki/File:Renoir-Monet_painting.png
On Passing Through the Morning Woods
A Boy Walking through a Danish Wood, Hans Agersnap (1857–1925)
https://commons.wikimedia.org/wiki/File:Hans_Agersnap_-_Dansk_skovparti_med_spadserende_dreng.png
Storm
Stormy Landscape, Rembrandt (1638)
https://commons.wikimedia.org/wiki/File:Rembrandt_Harmensz._van_Rijn_149.jpg
After the Storm: A Moment of Peace
Storm in the Mountains, Albert Bierstadt (1870)
https://commons.wikimedia.org/wiki/File:HRSOA_AlbertBierstadt-Storm_in_the_Mountains.jpg
Joy of Life
Rembrandt Laughing, Rembrandt (c.1628)
https://commons.wikimedia.org/wiki/File:Rembrandt_laughing_1628.jpg

IV. JOY OF THE SEASONS
Paysage, Berthe Morisot (1867)
https://commons.wikimedia.org/wiki/File:Berthe_Morisot_-_Paysage_(watercolour).jpg
Winter Moment
Author's Photograph

Together on a Snowy Path
Indian Woman Moccasin Seller, Cornelius Krieghoff (1815–1872)
https://commons.wikimedia.org/wiki/File:%27Indian_Woman_Moccasin_Seller%27,_oil_paintings_by_Cornelius_Krieghoff.jpg
Winter Celebration
The Christmas Tree, Albert Chevallier Tayler (1911)
https://commons.wikimedia.org/wiki/File:Albert_Chevallier_Tayler_-_The_Christmas_Tree_1911.jpg
Spring Awakening
Sous-bois, Paul Cézanne (c.1890)
https://commons.wikimedia.org/wiki/File:Sous-bois,_par_Paul_C%C3%A9zanne,_Yorck.jpg
A Stirring in the Soil
Spring Spreads One Green Lap of Flowers, John William Waterhouse (1910)
https://commons.wikimedia.org/wiki/File:John_William_Waterhouse_-_Spring_Spreads_One_Green_Lap_of_Flowers.JPG
Lovely as a Tree in Spring
Cherry Tree in Blossom, Edvard Munch (1905)
https://commons.wikimedia.org/wiki/File:Edvard_Munch_-_Cherry_Tree_in_Blossom_and_Young_Girls_in_the_Garden.jpg
Share with Me the Start of Summer
Summer Sunshine, Numa François Gillet (1868–1940)
https://commons.wikimedia.org/wiki/File:Summer_Sunshine_by_Numa_Fran%C3%A7ois_Gillet.jpg
On Greeting the Splendors of Autumn
A wooded path in autumn, H. A. Brendekilde (1902)
https://commons.wikimedia.org/wiki/File:H._A._Brendekilde_-_A_wooded_path_in_autumn_(1902).jpg
As Seasons Pass: Brief Is Life
From the U.S. Fish and Wildlife Service
https://commons.m.wikimedia.org/w/index.php?search=Polar+bear+cubs&title=Special:MediaSearch&type=image&haslicense=unrestricted

V. THE JOY OF CHILDREN
One Hundred Children in the Long Spring, Su Hanchen (c.1130–1160)
https://commons.m.wikimedia.org/wiki/File:One_Hundred_Children_in_the_Long_Spring-crop.jpg

First Moments
Birth, Hannah Hoch (1924)
https://commons.wikimedia.org/wiki/File:Birth_by_Hannah_Hoch,_1924,_oil_on_canvas_-_Germanisches_Nationalmuseum_-_Nuremberg,_Germany_-_DSC02359.jpg
Moments with My Grandchild
Child with a Dog, Francis Wheatley (1747–1801)
https://commons.wikimedia.org/wiki/File:Child_with_a_Dog_.PNG
Child's Garden
The Artist's Garden at Vétheuil, Claude Monet (1880)
https://commons.wikimedia.org/wiki/File:Claude_Monet,_The_Artist%27s_Garden_at_V%C3%A9theuil,_1881,_NGA_52189.jpg
Remembering Father's Garden
Picking Flowers in a Field, Mary Cassatt (1875)
https://commons.wikimedia.org/wiki/File:Mary_Cassatt_-_Picking_flowers_in_a_field_--_1875.jpg
Daughter
Author's Photograph
Son
Author's Photograph
Before School
Children's Games, Pieter Brueghel the Elder (c.1560)
https://commons.wikimedia.org/wiki/File:Pieter_Bruegel_the_Elder_-_Children%27s_Games_-_WGA3343.jpg
Recess
Dancing Children, Helen Sophia O'Hara (1900)
https://commons.wikimedia.org/wiki/File:Dancing_children,_by_Helen_Sophia_O%27Hara.jpg
Merry-Go-Round
Carousel, Vilmos Aba-Novák (1931)
https://commons.wikimedia.org/wiki/File:Aba-Nov%C3%A1k_Carousel_1931.jpg
Summer Dream
The Swimming Hole, Charles Courtney Curran (c.1894)
https://commons.wikimedia.org/wiki/File:The_Swimming_Hole_.jpg
Pup in Heaven
A Young Girl and Her Dog, Joshua Reynolds (c. 1780)
https://commons.wikimedia.org/wiki/File:Sir_Joshua_Reynolds_-_A_young_girl_and_her_dog.jpg

About the Author

Paul is an author of books, poems, progressive essays, and scientific journal articles. His most recent book of fiction was *Alice's Adventures*, published in 2022 by *Kelsay Books*. His historical novel, *1871: Rivers on Fire*, was self-published in 2021. His most recent non-fiction book was *Disposable Americans*, published in 2017 by *Routledge*.

Paul's website is:
BooksByPaulB.com

www.ingramcontent.com/pod-product-compliance
Lightning Source LLC
LaVergne TN
LVHW050539100826
845148LV00002B/621

* 9 7 8 1 6 3 9 8 0 3 6 3 7 *